YESTERDAY'S SUMMER

A Collection of Poems by
David Bowker

A.H. STOCKWELL
PUBLISHERS SINCE 1898

Published in 2023 by
David Bowker
in association with
Arthur H Stockwell Ltd
West Wing Studios
Unit 166, The Mall
Luton, Bedfordshire
ahstockwell.co.uk

British Library Cataloguing-in-Publication Data
A catalogue record for this book is available from the British Library.

ISBN: 9780722352793

To Aliza Batool,
for your kind words of encouragement

Contents

A Friday 1

A Trip to Gravelly Hill Interchange 2

A Walk in Scotland 8

Anything 9

Armchair 10

Beautiful Words 11

Become 12

Brand New Beggar 13

Catch you later 15

Colour 16

December, December 17

Do 18

Eyes 19

Flags 20

Home 21

Kiss 22

Nothing 23

Painting 24

Photograph 25

Please Sing, Yellow Bird 26

Rain 27

Robin 28

Running 29

Suburbs 30

Sun 31

Sunrise 32

Tree 33

Void 35

Weed 36

Yesterday's Summer 37

YESTERDAY'S SUMMER

A Friday

(2014)

You're waking up and the weekend is with you. Rising early and making that morning run around the block of darkened streets and yapping dogs, you're into the day, and stepping out of your streaming shower afterwards you're relishing the taste of reality, a tautness of fitness and feeling. Breakfasted and crossworded you're City Centre-bound. Taxi there and taxi back and you're home unpacking your produce, fridging it for safekeeping. Putting on the kettle, ready to relax, a biscuit or two or three or four and you're home and dry. Stretching ahead, the precious unchained hours are yours for the taking, for the savouring of tock tick tock from your bedside clock as the morning light first strengthens and then mellows as afternoon advances. You're being you, doing whatever you do, as the gift of day glides to touchdown with the coming of dusk. You're closing the curtains.

A Trip to Gravelly Hill Interchange

(1997)

A surprise,
even to see foliage
here.
I was expecting no more than
dumb, ugly concrete.
But summer breezes caress
leaves that lap
soothingly against your mighty
pillars, Spaghetti.
All that is needed is a
Corinthian flourish
and this temple to transport
would be complete.
You are a Colosseum
of car life, a concrete
and steel institution,
massive and manly, yet with feminine
curves that bend around the wide-angle
sky,
as I look upwards and follow your railed
and regular course.
Rollercoaster? Grand National? How many laps
have you witnessed?
The race never ends;
day and night. Do you ever sleep?

Standing, like a horse, perhaps.
I am lucky to find you in such
benevolent mood, Spaghetti, blue skies today
sparkle in the interstices of your
muscular limbs
and clouds high ahead, in slow motion,
move sure-footedly to their destination,
ever changing.
No rush, as they disappear behind your body,
and re-emerge.
They've been here before and will come
again.
The cycle of many seasons
never dulls their beauty, yet your
youthful exuberance is gone. Measure it in man-hours
or miles per hour or gallons consumed:
you burn the midnight oil, Spaghetti,
and awake to the song of the lark.
How many sunrises and how many sunsets
have you framed?
What winters have chilled your bones?
What summers have baked your limbs?

I take the subway path,
one of four
that converge on a strange oasis
beneath your mighty carcass. I stand and admire
your structure
as a cyclist silently glides past me
and the odd pedestrian, eyes to the ground,
potters along to somewhere else,
the pub perhaps.
Lunchtime: loneliness and leaves.
Shadows soon to lengthen. I spot the inevitable
graffiti
and am shocked, surprisingly,
that this place is defaced
with the spray of juvenile desire.
Looking up again as a breeze
sends a pile of slender saplings
helter-skelter to brush against your thighs,
Spaghetti.
Thunder, thump, whizz, hum!
Your sounds.
A stadium of motion,
pumping heart,
Pantheon of the English Midlands.

Form equals function.
Grind, roar, groan, grate!
These sounds are heard yet hidden.
Here, underneath,
I see nothing
but spaces, light and shade. Perspectives.
Celebration of car culture
is lifted above me, unseen
but thunder-hungry.
Anonymous.
Urgent!
A continuum of arterial flow,
richly-laden,
pressing for profit,
brute and uncaring.
Built by the hands of material culture, you
Spaghetti,
breathe the ethos of our time.
Keep the flow going.
English lorries, lovable box vans,
blue and cream buses, bus of heads,
red car,
lady with shades,
blue sky,
sexy.

You have a soul, shaped
as you are by man.
Condemned to be
silent, slow, speed, sky, signs.
Signs:
Copley Hill, Earth Moving Equipment,
Fort Shopping Park, One Way – blue sign, blue sky.
Layered living is your forte.
Such beautiful curves, lanes that lie
together,
sleeping partners,
cousins of the highway.
Shout, Spaghetti!
Scream, Spaghetti!
Can you take the strain? I'm listening.
Quietly
I look and listen. Your lazy
rounded pillars deceive me, Spaghetti.
What strains
weigh you down?
You make it look so easy. Mute
you are though,
seen but not heard.

I write
and the light changes. You, secure in form,
are a chameleon of colour. I imagine you
purple in the evening light.
Purple profile, yellow sky. Must be, some nights!
A theatre of space and form
that must be; a dramatic dusk with doorways
of column and lintel, like the entrance
to an Egyptian temple. Arid
and strong you are, Spaghetti.
Resilient!
Forgive me for having thought you ugly.
Now I know you a little, I say
neither spaghetti, nor a string of pearls.
Perhaps, one strong knot,
tying together the ropes of our motion
twentieth century-style
can define you best.

A Walk in Scotland

(2022)

A silence that can contain
all the sounds and screams
and agonies of the past
can be imagined,
present still in that air.
There as I walk, alone,
rucksacked and booted,
in Scotland's bonny hills.
And June's exquisite flowers,
fresh and fragrant,
yellow, purple and blue,
sprinkled amidst the greensward,
light my privileged path,
and belie the mournful memories.
How peaceful now, it is,
with gentle breeze
and birdsong sweet,
a place to praise
God's generous gift of nature.
That brutal passion,
those drumbeats of doom,
those griefs, those horrors, those wailings:
stilled.
I stop. I listen.
Haunted is the air.

Anything

(2022)

The vast skies,
the rocky mountain ranges,
the oceans and the seas,
the forests and the land,
the deserts with their sands,
the earth and its moon,
the planets, stars and space between,
the gases, the light and the galaxies,
the interstellar distances,
the urge to life in lifeless space,
the flesh and blood and heart and soul,
the past, the present and beyond,
the universe – or multiverse,
the consciousness that asks
'Why should there be anything?'

Armchair

(2022)

Empty armchair.
High-backed, winged,
floral-patterned.
Missing a person now.
She,
who sat in it,
body like a broken bird.
Frail.
Gnarled-fingered.
Eyes seeing only the past.
Vase of fresh flowers
perfuming the solitary room.
Photos of family
enough to make you weep.
Couple of books.
Her last room:
four walls and a bed.
A lived life.
Weekend visitors, yes.
The sound of receding footsteps,
fading voices, as they left.
Missing a person now.
Floral-patterned,
winged,
high-backed,
this empty armchair.

Beautiful Words

(2022)

caress
turquoise
lilac
peach
vanilla
verdant
vivacious
debonair
exquisite
viridian
epoch
velvet
luminescent
coalesce
dreamt
pristine
cornice
genre
key
quay
mauve
nuance
piquant
revolve
tambourine
purl
ambient
yearn
iridescence
magenta
jasmine
puissance
quash

Become

(2022)

I'm becoming what I thought
only others became.
The lifeless greying hair,
haloed around the balding crown;
the leathery skin,
with lines etched by experience;
the less hopeful eyes,
still blue but showing signs
of wear and tear;
the weaker stride,
not so sure-footed as in my youth;
the faltering strength
of arms and legs;
the set-in-my-ways routine,
of knowing what I like;
the ebbing away of belief,
in what I can now achieve;
the sense of time
speeding up with every passing year;
the loss of friendships,
getting down to the bare bones;
the feeling of being propelled
by some mighty force
to the finishing line.

Brand New Beggar

(2022)

Brand new beggar
Sitting in the street
Yesterday the good life
Now you're on your seat
Credit cards or cash
Anything will do
Beggars can't be choosers
The choice is not for you

Well-heeled worker
Striding down the street
Salary and bonus
All of yours to keep
No bad luck
Has yet to lay you low
As low as beggarman has gone
But fate plays tricks you know

Threatening rain cloud
Hanging in the sky
Washes down on beggarman
Now no longer dry
Clouds don't care for comfort
They'll soak you if they can
Cardboard home's a washout
Get plastic if you can

Friends and family members
Oh-so-far away
Contact truly broken
Misery's the price you pay
Alone and feeling helpless
Adrift in this bleak town
Succumb to sleep and squalor
Don't let it get you down

Voice of human kindness
Wakes you out of sleep
Cares for your condition
Can I get you something to eat?
A chicken tikka sandwich
Will see you through to noon
Accompanied by coffee strong
To lift the heavy gloom

Now you're on your feet and trudging
To some new likely spot
With blankets 'round your shoulders
'cause warm clothes you haven't got
It takes some time to find it
A place that's warm and dry
You ask how did I get here?
And want to weep and die

Brand new beggar
Lifeless in the street
Shrouded in your sleeping bag
Forever gone to sleep
No one there to mourn you
Most folk unaware
This never should have happened
If only we could care

Catch you later

(c. 1996)

Thoughts, events, emotions, ideas:
unwittingly conceived and perceived,
are steps that
take us
imperceptibly towards
our present.
They leave us grasping
for the unattainable,
the imagined innocence
of what
we never were.
They float
further and further
back,
a jumble
of clues stretched out,
a kind of code
going one way
whilst we go
the other.

Colour

(2022)

Above and beyond all words,
world within the world,
essence and energy,
revelation of light,
colour carries the glory of creation.
Mighty red, scorching and bleeding,
celestial blue, heaven's chamber,
sunshine yellow, lighting and lifting the spirits,
nature's green, soothing in myriad shades,
mysterious violet, pulsating dark down deep,
orange, oh orange, amazing intensely.
As life springs from light,
and light gives us colour,
so colour gifts us life.

December, December

(2015)

The news came with force, with velocity.
It rocked us out of our complacency.
I'm flabbergasted.
I can't believe I'm hearing this.
I don't know how these choices are made,
but out of a blue December sky
came the dreaded moment of truth,
of reality,
the cycle of change moving, unmoved,
and some of us swept along
out of the orbit of here and towards
some as yet unknown location.
Networks broken,
schedules rescheduled,
the next steps of your Adventure
are about to be trodden.
Tried and tested days and weeks
will be transformed
as your new existence takes shape.
You leave us and as you look back
only greater will grow the gulf
that separates us
as time takes you farther out
and we fade to a dim light.

Do

(2022)

Do nothing.
De-activate
and
sit becalmed.
Freeze all
motion.
Do
not think;
be.
Hear what
you
never heard.
Smell,
touch,
see,
feel
foreverness.

Eyes

(2022)

Strange to face
one's own eyes through
the medium of a mirror.
To be questioned.
Odd to be looked at
by yourself.
To be held to account.
Hard to be eyeballed
by eyes you
thought you knew.
To be confronted.
Weird to meet
another you,
reflected
face to face.
To be soul-searched.
Curious to gaze at
an image of self, inches away
but infinitely far.
To be toyed with.
Sobering to see
the lines and the tracks,
the crevices and creases
surrounding those eyes.
To be reminded.

Flags

(c. 1996)

Two proud flags
stationed in white
proximity,
barrel-chested,
arrogant,
brave and true,
demand my allegiance.
Sternly they strut;
red-rippled,
muscly,
cool,
unanswerable.
Carrying the charge
of deep-welled grief.

Home

(2022)

Home,
beating heart of my hopes,
foundation of my past and my present,
where would I be
without you?
My weary head I rest
within your willing walls.
Your bricks and mortar
and your black-gated garden of green
give sanctuary to my body and soul.
Golden memories stretch back years,
and moments of despair too.
Tears, joy, drama and all
the twists and turns of life,
are rooted in this quiet cul-de-sac,
in you, centre of my gravity.
Knower of my every need,
you nourish and sustain me.
Within you I dwell
as you dwell within my heart,
my humble abode.
Keeper of my restless energies,
always to you do I return,
from fields afar or from the town.
Home, my beating heart,
steady and loyal,
cherished and sacred are you.

Kiss

(2022)

We kiss,
and contentment
floods my brain
and body.
Rapture spreads
a warm delight,
lifting me high
to paradise.
I float.
Yet your animal breath
is earthen.
Clay we are, indeed,
and kisses as fugitive
as flesh,
but oh, that consummate moment!
Burning into my soul.

Nothing

(2022)

Nothing before, nothing after.
Is that the natural state
of your being?
Infinite time and space either side
of your breath of life?
This existence a blip?
Eternity bookending
your brief glow?
You came from where?
Bringing nothing.
You depart to where?
Taking nothing.

Painting

(2022)

The painting on the wall,
framed, silent,
presents itself to her,
full face.
Chroma to nourish her soul.
Yellow, red, blue, brown, black.
Oh, she wants greedily to eat
with her eyes
that rich assortment,
those sensitive placements
of buttery pigment.
Balm for her spirit,
a jigsawed colour carnival.
The real and imagined:
image and material.
A duality.
There the magic lies.
Soul-satisfying, eye-quenching.
Mind and matter
married, synthesised,
set before her hungry eyes.
Each shape, line, colour, tone
neighbour to another,
partners in a dance of harmony,
and the parts in blissful proportion
to the whole.
All held in by those four cardinal lines—
the edges of the image.
Outside of this is she,
but life pulses through her
as this painting feeds her need
for beauty, matter, spirit, mystery.

Photograph

(2022)

Stilled, your smiling face,
a world set in amber.
I hold your image in my hands,
fingers round the frame.
We look at each other,
unable to reach out and touch,
or reel in the years,
either of us.
That distance impossible to bridge.
Behind you trees, grass, flowers, clouds,
long since changed – or gone.
Dust now, no doubt.
Or transformed into new life.
That sun: older now,
as we all are,
ageing as we speak.
Seeming the same as ever, this photograph:
frame, glass, paper, image.
Yet it too succumbing to time.
Yellowing,
slowly evolving,
taking on a patina,
in my mind at least,
a crust of age,
changing with the seasons.
It'll be something quite different
to our descendants.

Please Sing, Yellow Bird

(2022)

Please sing, yellow bird,
in your winter willow tree,
for I so yearn to hear
the lilt of your sweet voice.
Sing for me, yellow bird,
lift me up
and I will love you.

Rain

(2022)

Saggy grisaille of watery cloud
slung across the sky
weeps its copious load,
tipping tapping, pitting patting, on my window pane.
Shrouded in gloom, inside and out,
the sky a sombre hue,
shadows deepening within my walls
match my murky soul.
Pooled and soaked, drenched and dripping,
outside the verdant view
is glazed with misty moisture,
so watery is the air.
And squally gusts that punch and pull
the willows in their prime
animate the dismal scene
with life's unceasing energy,
a counterpoint to sullen skies
whose droplets come, come, come,
bringing their melancholic plish plash
on my window pane.

Robin

(c. 1996)

A robin kindly visited my garden,
hairsbreadth legs, hopping
cheerfully, and of
careful eye.

Tender spot of colour,
cup-handed and of
beating breast,
playing in the privet,

animating January's bare
breath.
Pocket of playfulness
contained in a
frame,
bobbing and bopping.

Crushable
– not here, but children in
lion-like prowess
can be clumsy.

Twig-hidden then,
taking its leave with
no great ceremony,
vibrations of a branch
saw this cherub depart.

Running

(2022)

'Running' is a poem I have to write,
If only to express my long-running delight
In how I feel in body and mind,
Whilst stretching my legs, using all of my might.

The rhythm is part of the joy of the thing,
The metronome factor is what it can bring.
It builds and it builds and it carries you through,
You almost begin to feel like a king.

Round the course three times you might go,
You've done it before, each step fast or slow.
O'er cobbles and gravel, tarmac and soil,
There isn't a puddle or rise you don't know.

Your arms are a-punching, your heart is a-beating,
There may be a risk that you're overheating,
But years of your life have been spent in resisting,
And there's never a danger that you'll go down cheating.

A river of thoughts is your mind as you run,
Repetitive phrases return like the sun.
Ideas for titles of books you might write,
It's hard to explain from just where they have come.

Reaching the end is a moment so sweet,
You're shattered and ready to sit on that seat.
A feeling of having achieved once again,
You thank the good Lord and look down at your feet.

Suburbs

(c. 1996)

Parked buttock to breast in stewy suburbs,
fat-tyred cars graze like well-fed cows in a pasture,
and designer-clad children with chunky bicycles
circle, hero-focussed.
Tea time's yellowing air curdles,
dirty with the day's business.
The television's on for the night, blue-eyed,
cutting corners of light from window to window;
themed dreams channelled
for easy digestion, character-led, of
lives lived parallel to these.
Lives that revolve around revered lawns,
pea-green and sweet,
and regulation bedding plants,
June-cute and hose-thirsty,
that parade,
tantalised by England's
uncertain sun. Swish
of tyre on tarmac as a car
corners in third, leaves
our air heavy with the reek
of an aching sadness.

Sun

(2022)

Imperious sun,
arisen, as my life,
burn fierce,
light my path,
guide me
as the god you are.
Command me.
Brook no argument.
Illuminate my every step.
Traverse the heavens
at your will,
and I will bow down
to you.
Set your course,
and I will follow,
knowing you are there,
until your light is gone.
Then, at eventide, leave me, alone,
as you must.

Sunrise

(2022)

I prefer sunrise to sunset,
that fresh crimson promise
of pure day.
Crystalline, crisp,
washed of blemish and
blank-page gifted.
Lit from below.
Luminescent,
offering rebirth and
singing with renewal.
A clean slate,
serene in its simplicity.

Tree

(2022)

A tree says it all,
From winter to fall.
It shows us the truth,
Every bit of it, all.

Bare-branched winter bleak,
Big-leaved summer's peak,
It mirrors life's seasons,
Though each one's unique.

The root is its anchor,
Its port in a storm,
Holds tight through the rancorous
Gale-lashed morn.

The trunk that you've wanted
To hug with your love,
Is majestically holding
The parts up above.

The bough is a branch
That bends in the breeze,
How supple that limb,
In thee I believe.

The branch, the penultimate
Part of the tree,
Provides space and time
For the leaves that will be.

The leaf that emerges
So green in the spring,
Is life's affirmation,
To me everything.

Root, trunk, bough and branch,
Leaf, blossom and fruit,
Your glory's immutable
And epic to boot.

A tree says it all,
From winter to fall.
It spans generations.
We can learn from it all.

Void

(2022)

There's a void in my life right now, I say,
achingly real, something I feel,
painfully present, far from ideal.

There's a hole in your life right now, you say,
there when you wake up, start of the day,
always within you, work, rest or play.

There's a space in his life right now, he says,
space for reflection, on all he has lost,
shows him so clearly, too high is the cost.

There's a gap in her life right now, she says,
full of nostalgia, thoughts of the past,
making her fearful that nothing can last.

There's a chasm in our lives right now, we say,
it's empty and dark, not like before,
if this is our future, seems too much to endure.

There's a hollow in your lives right now, you say,
where once there was joy, once there was mirth,
laughter and sunshine, and all that was worth.

There's an absence in their lives right now, they say,
a windblown street, an empty park,
a dream that yet lingers, on which they still hark.

Weed

(2022)

Unwanted.
Ripped from the earth.
Flung to one side,
without a thought.
Your life sap fading
from that moment.
Worthless are you deemed,
an imposter without honour.
Fit only for the pyre.
Unworthy company
for flora more cherished
by those who pick and choose.
Uprooted, unearthed, unloved.
Sacrificed for the greater good.
Oh, weed.

Yesterday's Summer

(2022)

Now I notice more and more
from where I stand
this world moving away from me,
into the future,
as I, marooned in my ways,
slide away, unnoticed.
More people younger than me,
fewer older.
I edge towards obsolescence.
My concerns of no concern
to those of youthful heart,
my energies, though still intact,
palely imitate what they were in the past.
My books, my art, my taste in music,
all irrelevant.
I've had my day.
I've had my chance.
I'm yesterday's summer.

www.ingramcontent.com/pod-product-compliance
Lightning Source LLC
Chambersburg PA
CBHW021916040426
42447CB00007B/889